THE MANAGER'S

RESPONSIBILITY FOR

COMMUNICATION

THE MANAGER'S
RESPONSIBILITY FOR
COMMUNICATION

by John Garnett

The Industrial Society

First published 1964 by
The Industrial Society
Peter Runge House
3 Carlton House Terrace
London SW1Y 5DG
Telephone: 01–839 4300

Ninth edition 1989
© *The Industrial Society, 1964, 1983, 1989*

ISBN 0 85290 438 X

British Library Cataloguing in Publication Data
Garnett, John, 1921—
    The managers responsibility for communication.—9th ed
    1. Management . Communication
    I. Title II. Series
    658.4'5

Typeset by Columns Ltd, Reading
Printed and bound in Great Britain by Belmont Press, Northampton

CONTENTS

FOREWORD

Whatever the discipline or level of management, the responsibilities of managers are many and various. It is their job to produce results with essentially just two resources— people and time.

To maximise the potential of both, most managers need some reminders and basic guidelines to help them.

The Notes for Managers series provides succinct yet comprehensive coverage of key management issues and skills. The short time it takes to read each title will pay dividends in terms of utilising one of those key resources— people.

The success of managers depends, primarily, on their ability to communicate to all the people for whom they are responsible, what they need to do, and the importance of doing it.

If success is to be achieved, there is also a need to harness the ideas, views, and experiences of people actually carrying out the job.

This booklet is filled with practical examples and is an essential aid for every manager.

ALISTAIR GRAHAM
Director, The Industrial Society

1

WHY DOES
COMMUNICATION MATTER

It matters because failures in communication are costly.

Example 1.
In a production job where a new manager was appointed, but all other variables were the same, a saving of 5 per cent was achieved, amounting to £80,000 per annum, because the new manager laid down an effective system of communication. The main difference, as far as the employees were concerned, was that under the new manager they knew what the problem was, what they were trying to achieve, how he wanted the problem tackled and what part they had to play in order to get improvements. They knew, too, the extent to which they succeeded in reaching the individual targets set.

Example 2.
Out of 35 stoppages in a large organisation, eighteen were due to failures of communication. The cost of these stoppages could not be measured in the hours lost alone; the stoppages upset the whole rhythm of production and lessened co-operation between employees and their managers.

Where there is change, the full benefits can only be achieved where there is an adequate communication system for explaining face-to-face, directly to employees, what is required, and why.

Example 3.
A large company negotiated centrally a productivity deal with the unions, to achieve greater flexibility in the use of manpower. In practice, the only sections of the company that succeeded in getting the flexibility were those with a direct and systematic method of communication, through managers and supervisors, to their own employees.

Adequate communication results in greater productivity through more effective work and greater co-operation.

Example 4.
An organisation in the City gets a measurable increase in staff productivity following each monthly briefing by management to the staff. Progress against local targets, and the priorities for the coming month, are explained.

Executives with good potential will leave the staff if they are unaware of their prospects within the company. Finding and training a successor is costly; it will have repercussions in the section and it lowers morale among colleagues. Failures in communication are not limited to factories or to shop-floor level.

There is no monopoly of wisdom at the top of organisations. We cannot afford to waste the ideas and inventiveness of employees at any level.

Example 5.

A company set up a formal consultative system to tap these ideas at shop-floor level. One employee with 30 years' service suggested using a domestic oven cleaner to prepare some of the surfaces used in production. It solved a long standing problem. When asked why he had not suggested it before, he answered that management had given no indication that they wanted employees' views.

We need to bear in mind that the new generation of employees is much more used to being involved – at school, college or university – and they therefore expect that involvement to continue at work.

People will only give of their best if they fully understand the decisions that affect them and the reasons behind those decisions. People need to understand:

- what they have to do and why
- how they are performing against budgets and set targets
- what their conditions of employment are.

They can then be involved in what they are doing, resulting in greater efficiency, higher morale, and greater co-operation.

The need for a properly organised system of communication applies as much in offices, research laboratories, drawing offices and hospitals as it does on the shop floor. If effective communication is to be achieved, it cannot be left to casual methods.

2

WHAT TO COMMUNICATE

The first things to decide are our priorities, because the conclusions will affect the communication method to be used. Clearly, you cannot tell everybody everything—or consult everyone on everything, otherwise no other work would be done.

The normal approach has been to try to tell people what their managers think will be of *interest* to them, omitting those things they must understand whether they are interested in them or not. Such a yardstick is misleading; it results in much of secondary importance being explained.

Example 6.

The end use of a product from another works may be of some interest to employees. On the other hand, in times of industrial peace, the dispute procedure may be of no interest at all. To communicate the first point is of no great importance. To communicate the second is vital, for once a dispute is on, it is too late to try to explain the need to keep to procedures.

If employees are not interested it will be more difficult – but no less vital – for management to get them to understand.

This understanding is also the first step in achieving successful consultation with employees. Too often, managers seek ideas and opinions in formal consultation structures without having first given employees that understanding of the work from which realistic ideas and opinions can come.

First principles

The priority, then, is for managers to communicate *under-standing* of those matters that significantly affect a person's will to give the best of their work. People do not have to agree in order to co-operate with a decision, but they must understand how and why it has been made.

What are these matters which must be understood?

Things that affect a person's job

- What is the job?
- Who is my boss?
- What contribution does my work make to the total job?
- Where does the work come from and go to? What is it? What is the end product? What is it for?
- What are my work targets? To what extent are they being achieved? What are the standards?
- To what extent can I influence costs?
- What are the safety standards?
- What changes are being made and why?
- What are the priorities in my work over the next month?

Things that affect a person's employment

- What is the rate of pay? How are salaries or wages calculated? What is the basis for the bonus? What are the arrangements for overtime pay?
- What are the holiday arrangements?
- What is the sick pay?
- How do I get promoted? How do supervisors get selected?
- What is the length of notice? Are there any redundancy arrangements?
- What are the negotiating procedures? How do I make a suggestion or a complaint? Where can I get help with personal problems?
- What is the company's attitude to my membership of a trade union?
- What changes are being made and why?

Some argue that many such matters cannot be communicated because there are no understandable reasons for the policy decisions taken. In the vast majority of cases this is untrue and is merely a further example of communication failure by senior management. If only the person who took the decisions and decided the policy can be discovered, it will normally be found that they took them for reasons that are understandable.

3

WHICH METHOD TO CHOOSE

All methods of communication in industry and commerce can be grouped under three headings.

- *Managers and supervisors*: Face-to-face communication by the manager or supervisor.

- *Representatives*: communication through the representative, who may be a member of the staff committee, a shop steward, a staff representative on the employee council, the production committee, the safety committee, or a fellow worker.

- *Mass methods*: a person being informed through reading the noticeboard, company newspaper and magazine, manager's newsletters, booklets, circulars, attending mass meetings (when more than 40 people are involved), receiving a popular version of the company's annual report, hearing loudspeakers, using phone-in programmes, seeing films and closed circuit television.

Managers must decide which method of communication is to be used and be clear about what each can do and its limitations. Much of what goes wrong in communication is caused by managers not having thought out clearly what each method can achieve.

Managers and supervisors

Strengths

- The manager or supervisor, as the representative of management to the work group in the office or on the shop floor, is the appropriate person to explain the most important matters listed on pages 5 and 6, because these things result from managerial decisions or, in the case of negotiated matters, from joint management/union decisions.

- Part of the job of being a leader is to be the person to whom people look for explanations about things that matter. By becoming the communicator the manager or supervisor will become a more effective leader.

- Supervisors can tailor their explanations to suit the particular group and, following the explanation, questions can be asked. What needs to be explained to one group will be different for another. The opportunity to ask questions is vital for understanding.

- Much of what must be communicated is already common knowledge to the manager. For example, the reasons for a change in production plans which affect a person's job.

- Face-to-face communication with the group saves time, ensures common understanding, and is the most powerful method of 'selling' ideas and building group commitment.

Weaknesses

- With a line of leadership of more than two levels between the top manager and the person on the shop floor or in the office, communication by this method does not happen adequately unless organised.

- Unless planned, it can be expensive in terms of management time.

- The line of leadership cannot, alone, adequately handle upward communication. The top of an organisation is seldom aware of the vividness of attitudes at the bottom if what is reported to them has been passed through a number of levels of the hierarchy.

Representatives

Strengths

- They provide an opportunity for management to explain a policy directly to a few of the employees affected, saving much repetition at different levels.
- They are a necessity for adequate upward communication and invaluable in bringing home to senior management the vividness of feeling in the office or factory.
- The formal contact in representative meetings can and does bring an increase in informal contact.

Weaknesses

- Although management's explanations get over to the representatives, they normally fail to pass on the explanations satisfactorily to their constituents, particularly when the decisions are unpleasant. This is because the representatives of the employees find themselves trying to act as the representatives of management in explaining management policies. This is not the representative's job and puts them, as well as the supervisor, in an impossible position.
- If shop stewards are the main communicators they, not the supervisors, will become the leaders and bosses of the work group.

Mass methods

Strengths

- They offer the cheapest way of giving particular information to large numbers of people.
- They are quick, e.g. loudspeaker, notice at the exit.
- It is possible to ensure that the information transmitted is accurate.
- They are a necessary aid in support of communication through management.

Weaknesses

- Mass methods are not good for transmitting understanding because you cannot ask a noticeboard or a letter a question. In theory, you can ask a question at a mass meeting; in practice the majority of British people will not do so in meetings of more than 20.
- Although the information transmitted is accurate, it does not necessarily follow that it is accurately received.
- The most important matters to be understood are those that affect the individual or working group. These need separate explanations for each group and the mass method can only cover the general aspect.

Using the grapevine

No mention has been made of communication by rumour (the grapevine). It exists, but managers use it at their peril. The grapevine will pass facts accurately—sometimes, as in the case of an appointment, before the decision has been made! But it always puts forward an *uncharitable reason* for the decision. The grapevine *always* passes the 'why' in terms that are bad for co-operation. 'X has got the job and you know *why* that is.'

A grapevine withers in those organisations where people know that there is a systematic way of learning about the things that matter from the supervisors or managers.

The importance of questions

In considering the strengths and weaknesses of the various means of communication, stress has been laid on the importance of providing the opportunity for people to ask questions if understanding is to be achieved.

Today, many people think that if you write something clearly enough, people will understand. There is all the difference between providing the information and getting people to understand. Experience of everyday life shows that face-to-face communication must take place and the opportunity to ask questions must be given before understanding will be obtained. Explanation to a small group affected will be more effective than to individuals. In the group, each person will benefit from the answers to another's questions.

Example 7.

An engineer who wants her draughtsmen to understand what she wishes them to design will not rely on putting instructions on paper. She will go and see the draughtsmen and tell them face-to-face. After questions, some of which will merely involve repetition of what she has already said, the draughtsmen will understand. The engineer can then confirm the instructions in writing.

Summary

When choosing a method of communication, recognise that any systematic method is better than none at all. The mass method is the easiest to work. The hardest is through managers and supervisors. But communication up and down will not be satisfactory in a large organisation without some use of all three methods, and the most important task will be making it work through managers and supervisors. The steps that must be taken by managers to make this method work adequately are explained in the next chapter.

4

EFFECTIVE
COMMUNICATION
THROUGH MANAGERS
AND SUPERVISORS

All members of management – including, of course, supervisors and foremen – must be made to appreciate the importance and benefits of adequate communication. The busier their working lives, the more necessary a systematic drill becomes. They cannot afford to leave communication to casual or *ad hoc* methods.

Example 8.

In an organisation, the decision of the works manager to change the production rate was passed down to the deputies and section leaders at their weekly meetings. Thereafter, it was left to casual explanations down the line of command and the reasons for the change were lost in the conglomeration of plant managers, super-intendents, foremen and supervisors. This resulted in the changes being made because: 'They had decided,' or it was a 'management decision'. This happens in works, offices, hospitals, building sites and government departments up and down the country and discourages hard work.

That 'they' gave it is reason for obeying an order, but not necessarily for co-operating with it. *The difference between co-operation and obedience is often the difference between profit and loss.*

If communication down through line management is to be effective, it must be systematic. The object is to ensure that employees have the decisions that affect their job or conditions of employment explained to them face-to-face by their immediate boss. Two steps are needed. First, establish a drill for team briefing that ensures communication right down the line to the work group, through supervisors. Second, ensure that the necessary information is known by managers.

Team Briefing

Team briefing is simply a systematic drill to ensure communication takes place. Each department or section will organise its system of team briefing differently, depending on the number of people involved, the different levels, and the work arrangements, i.e. shifts. The drill for each group must be written down and made known to everyone in the group.

The crucial element is that the information briefed to the group should be relevant to that group. The drill that ensures this happens is that all briefers prepare the local items that need to be briefed, before receiving a briefing from their immediate manager. So at each level, the brief from above is being added to an existing local brief.

Example 9.

The individual foremen in a large engineering company write their own briefs on the first Tuesday in each month, the items being such things as work in progress on that line, the need to complete job cards each day, and the proposed finishing date for the new canteen. They then give their briefs to their departmental managers who read them and suggest additions as necessary. On the Thursday, all department managers brief their supervisors with the brief from above. The supervisors then add this to their local brief, and brief their teams on Thursday afternoon.

Briefing structure

A typical structure for briefing would be for a director, having been briefed by the board, to brief the works manager, who would in turn call the deputies and section heads together and brief them. The section heads then brief the foremen who go on to brief the shop floor. At this level, at least two thirds of the information being briefed by the foremen should be 'local', to do with the job that the group is doing. Local information could include: items collected since the last briefing; procedures that people need to be reminded of; and, very important, a local breakdown of company performance, i.e. the group's output against target, quality record, safety record and absenteeism record. Here, local relevant yardsticks should be used.

In this way, five levels of management can be covered in three steps. In some organisations it might be possible to get the whole management team together at one meeting, but the groups should be no larger than 15. Understanding of policies and decisions is only achieved if the group is small enough to allow questions and discussion: 15 is normally the maximum.

It is important that where information has to go through more than three levels of management, a written brief is prepared and a briefing folder is kept. For three levels or less, note-taking may be sufficient. *Briefers must be made to make notes*. This is vital.

Briefing routine

It is also important that the drill becomes an accepted part of a manager's and supervisor's job, and it is remembered that team briefing is communication with the work group by a management spokesman, not just to a selected few. It is management's job to communicate management's message, and it is vital, particularly at the lower levels, that this is done by the team leader (boss). Communication targets can be written into job descriptions and specifications.

WHEN?

Management must decide when briefing sessions should be held. In the case of day workers, this is often done following the lunch hour. Shift workers may be brought in early or held late and paid overtime. A more economic method is to hold over or bring in the shift supervisor. This often prevents communication failures between shift supervisors. Office and shop workers are briefed either first thing in the morning or just before closing time. Where none of these is possible, some companies find it necessary to bring people in on a Saturday morning. It has been found that where such arrangements have been made, the people concerned have appreciated the fact that they have had things properly explained to them. Perhaps the best situation, in the case of a widely scattered sales force, is to post the brief, then follow it up by a telephone call.

FREQUENCY

For briefing to be credible, it must be regular, with dates set aside in the diary. This also ensures that communication does not only happen in times of crisis. Many companies have found that monthly is the best frequency: most relevant figures are produced monthly and, at many levels, monthly meetings take place already and briefing can be incorporated into these. Another benefit is that the work group knows when the next briefing will be and will often wait to hear management's view of things before reaching conclusions. Also, one briefing is firmly established, should there be a vital message to pass on quickly, the system can be used at a moment's notice.

SUBJECTS

The subjects covered by the manager will be the decisions and policies which affect people's will to work. The four main headings are: *progress* (how the section is doing); *people*; *policy*; *points for action and the priorities in the coming month*. Local subjects and matters must be predominant at all levels, as well as examples of how major decisions affect a particular work group. This ensures that the majority of the information is relevant to the work group. The relevance of information at each level of briefing is vital (*see* Appendix 3).

HOW LONG?

Team briefing sessions should normally last not more than half an hour. A useful guide is for the supervisor to spend two-thirds of the time explaining management decisions and policies that affect those present, leaving one-third of the time for questions on the matters that have been briefed.

WHO TAKES THE BRIEFING SESSION?

Normally the foreman, or section head in the office. If people have difficulties in doing this (and this happens less often than managers think), they should be given some practice in:

- the skills of briefing
- writing a local brief
- delivering the brief
- handling questions and feedback.

Deputies able to 'act in absence', etc. should also be appointed to cover sickness, absence, holidays, and so on.

MONITORING

Systems only work when checked. A co-ordinator should be appointed who is accountable for the smooth running of the system. However, the success of the system depends on the commitment shown by managers at all levels to making it work.

All those running team briefing groups should note in their special folders the time of starting and ending, who was absent, and a one word description of what was discussed, e.g. progress, time-keeping, quality, reorganisation. There are no minutes and no agendas, but the more senior managers should 'walk the job' and ask people what they know about a point briefed. Indeed, they should also sit in on at least one first-line brief each year.

GETTING STARTED

First, senior management must be committed to the system of briefing. Second, all briefers at each level must understand the system, and its benefits. A two day training course is the best way to gain their commitment and give them some basic instruction in briefing. Thirdly, the first few briefs should not contain controversial subjects.

Where there has been no tradition of the supervisor or manager talking to the working group, some planning will be needed to get it started. It can start as a training session on doing the job better. A lead-in may be achieved as a result of something not being properly explained, followed by a subsequent request for correct information. The introduction of safety talks is another starting point. As confidence is achieved, the subjects will extend to cover the job, promotion policies, and finally, after consultation and with the shop stewards playing their part, joint management/ trade union matters.

Summary

The main argument against taking such systematic steps as these is that we cannot afford the time. Where time studies have been made of a supervisor's duties, a very high proportion (80 per cent) is accounted for by communication. The time involved at shop floor level is less than 0.05 per cent of working time each month.

The systematic method as set out will shorten this time, not lengthen it. Most important of all, where supervisors have shouldered this leadership function of explaining to their working group the matters that affect them, they have been found to become more effective managers.

Getting Information to Line Managers

Certain information, about personnel policies in particular, must be fed into the line of leadership accurately and speedily. Most of the other information is there already. A management bulletin will be required, which can be distributed at a few hours' notice on a prearranged distribution list to each manager and supervisor, whenever some decision affecting large numbers of employees has been taken.

The management bulletin should state briefly what has been decided and the main reasons for the decision; as, for example, with details of trade union settlements, changes in a staff job, the introduction of a new way of working.

Each manager and supervisor should receive an individual copy of the management bulletin and not just be placed on a circulation list, since this may result in their hearing important information many days later. It is false economy to restrict the number of copies circulated.

Only urgent matters should be included in the bulletin, otherwise there will be a tendency for it to be put at the bottom of a reading pile.

The bulletin must also state whether the information is to be communicated further and if so—how?

Example 10.

The intermediate results of a round of wage negotiations are circulated in the management bulletin to all managers and supervisors within 24 hours of the negotiation meeting ending. In this way, first line managers are as well and as quickly informed as the trade union representatives and the employees.

5

MAKING BETTER USE OF
EMPLOYEES' KNOWLEDGE

Effective communication of ideas and opinions upward from employees to management is essential for all organisations who seek full efficiency. At one end of the scale is the system of representatives and consultative committees; at the other is the local level problem solving team. Both types of consultation improve efficiency and increase the employers' sense of involvement.

Making better use of representatives and consultative committees

Direct discussions between employees and senior management are essential if managers are to be aware of the attitudes and feelings of those who will be affected by management decisions. Without such discussions, wrong decisions can, and do, result. Except in very small companies, some systematic committee meeting with elected representatives is necessary. To look on the committee as a sop to the workers or as a waste of management time is to miss an opportunity to increase efficiency and to take a proven step forward in any participation policies.

Purpose and function of a consultative committee

It is not the purpose of a consultative committee to put over management policy; that is the job of managers and supervisors in team briefing. Its purpose is:

- to give employees a chance to improve decisions by contributing comments *before* decisions are made
- to make the fullest possible use of their experience and ideas in the efficient running of the enterprise
- to give management and employees the opportunity to understand each other's views and objectives at first hand.

The main function of the committee is:

- to discuss, before decisions are taken, any matter affecting the efficiency of the enterprise and the interests of employees to which representatives can contribute.

Subjects for discussion

There should be no limitation on the subjects discussed except for:

- matters which can genuinely be called trade secrets
- matters which should be settled directly between employees and their immediate supervisor
- matters covered in union agreements if the committee is non-union.

The last limitation is a serious one because it prevents the committee from dealing with a whole range of subjects which are of immediate importance to employees. It is therefore a great advantage if the employee members of a committee are union representatives, so that there is no such restriction on topics for discussion. This does not mean that the committee becomes a negotiating body. Even in cases where the same committee is responsible for negotiation and consultation, the two processes are best kept separate, and the chairman should make sure that the committee understands what it is doing at any one time.

The following are examples of subjects which can be the concern of consultative committees:

- output and productivity, e.g. improvements in work methods, office planning, central services, design of machines, transport, office equipment
- manpower policies and procedures, e.g. principles of promotion
- education and training, e.g. induction of new employees, the training of young people
- safety, e.g. investigation of the causes of accidents
- selection and training of supervisors
- effectiveness of communication.

In addition, a committee which is union-based will be in a position to discuss, before negotiations take place:

- wage systems
- job evaluation
- hours of work
- holidays and holiday pay.

Agenda

This should be circulated in advance, with supporting information. More than half the agenda should be initiated by management. It is helpful to have one major subject at each meeting; this is best introduced at the previous meeting so that representatives have time to go away and think about the issues involved and discuss them with colleagues. Major items should also be introduced at the briefing meeting so that everyone knows that the subject is coming up for discussion.

All agendas should include an item which allows the chairman to talk about the progress of the works or office or department. This is not with a view to it being passed on, but to remind representatives of the organisational background against which they are talking.

Representatives

There is no need to have an equal number of representatives from each side. A membership of not more than 16 will produce a good committee; with such a number it should consist of about 11 elected representatives and five appointed representatives. It may be better to re-elect half the elected representatives each year. There should be a minimum service requirement for standing as a candidate; perhaps one year.

If the firm recognises trade unions, then the elected representatives should emerge through the union machinery in the organisation. It is best to include the shop stewards as representatives wherever possible.

The appointed representatives should consist of: the chairman, who should be the manager of the unit; there should always be a supervisor sitting as one of the management-appointed representatives; there should be someone who is a senior manager; and someone who is representative of the younger managers. The latter should be selected for ability and potential; this person will un-doubtedly embarrass management by their contributions, from time to time, but their presence on the committee will do more good than harm.

If an additional appointed representative is desirable, a person might well be chosen from a group which is not represented as a result of the elections.

Constituencies

Constituencies for the elected representatives should be drawn in such a way as to produce the maximum community of interest in the group concerned. In case of doubt, it is better to draw them on the basis of the job being done, rather than on the status of the group, e.g. it will be better to have a representative for the whole of the de-greasing plant or pension department, rather than to have one representative for the clerical workers employed throughout the organisation.

Meetings

Committees should meet at least every two months if they are to make a useful contribution. Provision should be made to allow for special additional meetings to be held when required.

Reporting back

Representatives may need assistance to communicate the outcome of consultative meetings. Minutes on the notice-board alone are not satisfactory. More can be achieved by supplying some or all of the following.

- A committee news-sheet immediately following the meeting. The committee news-sheets are not minutes and briefly cover only the most important items discussed. Within 24 hours, copies should be placed on pick-up racks at clocking stations, office entrances and canteens. People can then take a copy for themselves. If a newsletter exists, it may be possible to use this instead of the committee news-sheet. Publication dates must then be tied up satisfactorily with the consultative committee or committees.

- An occasional statement of what has been said for representatives to distribute among their own con-stituents. This is not as satisfactory as the news-sheet, although it may be easier to accomplish.

- Coaching in speaking for representatives. Four hours' practice with an effective speaker can make a real difference.

- An allotted time for reporting back.

- Management briefing of the decisions taken after consultation, stating that consultation has taken place.

Local level problem solving

Consultative committees, by their very structure, are limited to discussing overall company topics. Specific problems to do with the actual task in individual departments are best dealt with locally.

First line managers should regularly meet with their teams (or volunteers from their teams) to identify and solve their own local work-related problems. This will:

- reinforce the role of the first line manager
- encourage employees to use knowledge and ingenuity to make their areas more efficient
- 'crunch' local problems earlier rather than clogging up the consultative committee.

Many companies have made this step beyond consultative committees, using small, local, problem-solving meetings either on the local manager's own initiative or by installing quality circles.

Example 11.

A team of problem solvers on a battery line looked at a newly installed conveyor belt. They presented suggestions to the management. These ranged from filing down the corners of the safety barriers so as to prevent the operators' hands being cut, to filling up the areas between the bench and the belt and so reducing the scrap level.

6

MASS METHODS

Of all mass methods of communication, the most effective
are: noticeboards; company magazines and newspapers—
including the annual report to employees; the manager's
newsletter; employee handbooks; loudspeaker systems;
phone-in arrangements; and mass meetings.

Noticeboards

Location is important. They should be where people not
only pass, but can also stop to read, e.g. by entrances to
plants, offices, canteens.

There should be either two noticeboards, or one board
divided into two. One section can then be clearly labelled
and used only for urgent and new notices. Once a notice
has been on this section for 48 hours, it should be moved to
the other section (if it is of interest for more than a few days)
where notices can be left for reference.

A particular person should be made responsible for each
noticeboard. It is best if this person can be the departmental
supervisor.

Notices should be signed by an individual, rather than by
some legal entity such as the XYZ Company, which makes
people feel they are part of an impersonal web.

When drafting a notice, managers should bear in mind
how they would tell the contents to a person face-to-face on
the shop floor or in the office.

Company magazines and newspapers

The purpose of company magazines and company news-papers should be:

- to provide a mass means of explaining the company's activities and policies to its employees
- to help employees feel that they are involved in the company
- to create an atmosphere in which change is accepted.

When budgeting and planning company publications, the emphasis should be on frequency and flexibility. It goes without saying that small, casual, inexpensive (e.g. sten-cilled) newsletters are more topical and urgent than glossy magazines. Ideally, publication should be weekly or fort-nightly. Too often, the strict scheduling necessary for the production of glossy magazines inhibits topicality.

The prestige magazine can be sent to an employee's home and is sometimes charged for at a nominal rate. The newsletter should be free: the content should be such that employees need it and will read it, in which case it is in the management's interest to make it as available as possible.

The pick-up racks already mentioned for distributing the committee news–sheet, can be used for ordinary issues of the newspaper or newsletter.

Space in company newspapers should be divided into thirds: one-third for the product and other news that affects a person's job; one-third for developments or changes in conditions of employment; and one-third for social events. The third devoted to news that affects jobs will already have been communicated to those directly concerned* by their managers and supervisors. Repetition here serves to keep informed those less directly concerned.

Sometimes the magazine is also used as a public relations contact with customers, but it is better to have a completely separate publication for this.

The manager's newsletter

In large organisations where the newspaper covers a wide group of activities, there may be a need for some arrangement whereby the head of department, or works manager, can communicate, in writing, to all employees in their part of the organisation. Invaluable assets are the works manager's or department head's newsletter which goes to all employees, (including members of management) on the site or in the department.

Once more, it is essential that this newsletter appears frequently: at least monthly. Items should not be saved up; when there is something to be said, the newsletter should be sent out. It is a false economy not to run off enough copies for each person or merely to put the newsletter on a noticeboard.

Other advantages of a manager's newsletter between the senior manager and employees are:

- at times of stress and misunderstanding, there is a recognised method of confirming facts in writing
- there is no need to send letters about company matters to people's homes, or to use the pay packet to tell people about things that have little to do with pay; both means of communication are resented.

Accountability charts

People must know who is their boss and who is their boss's boss. There should be available, for each person, a copy of the accountability chart of their department or section, showing the boss's name and who is directly accountable to them. Unlike an organisation chart, it does not attempt to show the complexities of inter-relationships.

Employee handbooks

Each employee should receive an employee handbook setting out the main rules and arrangements that apply to them. The book should be as brief as possible, but it can be supplemented by booklets dealing with specific subjects, such as job evaluation schemes, the disputes procedure with the union, the sick pay scheme and pension fund.

These booklets should preferably be written in the form of questions and answers which explain specific aspects of conditions of employment. It may be obligatory, for instance, to provide employees with the rules of the pension fund in a legal form, but since this will be virtually unintelligible to anyone who is not an actuary or a lawyer, it will also be necessary to provide employees with an explanatory booklet in everyday language. In the case of works rule-books, a useful form is to set the rule out on one page and on the facing page give the reasons for the rule.

Loudspeaker systems

The great danger of these is that they tend to be used too much. They are not satisfactory for putting over a policy as the listener cannot even see the person speaking, let alone ask any questions. Loudspeaker systems cannot take account of the mood or the particular occupation of the listener.

Phone-in

Some large organisations adopt a phone-in system whereby any member of staff can phone an internal number and hear a recorded tape about current activities, sales position, or the reasons behind other news. Some adopt a system whereby a person can ask a question which is recorded and an answer provided.

Mass meetings

Mass meetings are valuable as the only practical way for people to hear the most senior managers directly. They are not good for getting understanding, principally because people will not ask questions; they are no substitute for the team briefing sessions.

Example 12.

A mass meeting is held once a year by a director or works manager, to explain to employees the results of the year's working and to talk about plans for the following year. Steps are taken to make it as easy as possible for shift to attend. It is held in the canteen at the end of the normal working day. Such meetings may draw about 40 per cent of the operatives and 70 per cent of the office staff.

In one organisation, the chief executive will speak each year at the time of the annual results, to 500 senior managers. It is then possible to require each of these managers to speak to similar numbers. This two-tier method of mass communication can be a valuable means of explaining the accounts. It can be supported by a video recording of the first meeting, but the video tape must be accompanied by a manager to deal with the questions that arise.

Annual report for employees

The publication of the annual report of the company gives a major opportunity to help people to understand the vital importance of their work. More and more companies issue a special report setting out the main facts and this provides the opportunity to explain that, during the year, people in the organisation have together created five different things:

- they have produced a certain volume of goods and services for other people
- they have generated the incomes of those employed, thus giving people freedom of expenditure
- they have provided tax revenue, both on those incomes and directly, which pays for social needs such as schools, hospitals and pensions
- they have generated saving in reserve for future development
- they have generated a return on people's saving in distributed profits.

Employee reports can also include information about employees, such as length of service, safety, and absenteeism statistics, and time lost through industrial disputes. These are particularly relevant if figures are compared from region to region, or department to department. Other helpful details to include concern:

- customers—who and where they are
- products—what brand names they appear under; what goods will they be part of; which sites make/deal with the various products/services the company offers

It is important that, when employee reports give figures, they include comparisons and comments. Bald figures tend to produce the reaction: 'So what?' unless it is clear whether or not management is pleased with the results and why the results are better or worse than expected.

The effectiveness of the employee report depends on how it is distributed. Experience suggests it is best distributed in a briefing or before a mass meeting, like the one described in the example earlier. This ensures that everyone receives the report and has a chance to ask questions. Many organisations post reports to employees' home addresses: this is the next best thing as everyone at least receives the report—but it does not encourage them to ask questions or discuss the report with colleagues.

Other mass methods

Other mass visual aids are posters, filmstrips, films, videos, and closed circuit television. All are most effective when they are used as an aid to face-to-face communication.

Example 13.
A company makes an annual video showing company financial results. This is shown to the shop floor in small groups by their supervisor in one of the monthly team briefing sessions. In this way, there is ample opportunity for questions, and the local implication of company performance can be explained.

Written communications and other mass methods can never become the main vehicle for communication. This must be done face-to-face using team briefing or consultative committees. The written word, etc. is therefore a useful back-up or a support document, and not the main or only vehicle.

7

IS COMMUNICATION
WORKING?

As in all aspects of management, it is necessary to check.

Walking the job

The simplest method is to ask questions, when walking round offices or factories, about why someone is doing a particular job or why a change has been made. If the explanation is inaccurate, or if the person does not know, the manager should take the matter up with the person's manager or supervisor.

Using consultative committees

After a major change has been made, discuss in the consultative committee whether the communication aspect has been adequately carried out and how it can be improved.

Using courses

Take the opportunity provided by training courses for managers and supervisors (the nearest thing to privileged occasions) for checking the adequacies of communication.

Instituting an investigation

Give a young person, such as a management trainee, the job of examining communication. This is best done by the investigator asking senior management for two or three examples of recent decisions which affect employees and tracking these decisions and the reasons behind them through all levels. Who did the managers talk to? When? How? How did the next level hear? When? How? It is important to note not only if the decision gets lost, but at what point the reasons have changed or become unknown.

Commissioning a written survey

There are two ways of doing this. A group of people may be asked in a questionnaire how they were informed of a particular recent decision: through the supervisor, company newspaper, manager's newsletter, noticeboard, representative, or by rumour? This usually reveals clearly how many people heard by rumour.

The second method is the attitude survey, where employees are asked, with great regard to anonymity, carefully designed questions about what they know of various policies and what their attitude is to their conditions, supervisors, managers and jobs. Many companies have found that this type of survey can be carried out most successfully by an outside body, as the employees are often reluctant to talk in detail to other employees about their problems, etc.

In both cases, the written surveys can produce some surprisingly quantitative illustrations of communication failures.

8

CONCLUSION

There is one common and vital factor in all the situations we face at work: the ability of every leader, be they manager or supervisor, to obtain the commitment of people to their work.

We know that a key factor in the leadership of our own bosses in this participative age is the extent to which they pay serious attention to communication both upward and downward. People achieve more, working for a leader who bothers with communication. This is true of each one of us who, as a leader of one or many, has responsibility for achieving people's co-operation.

If we take action to make communication happen, then, like others before us, we shall find efficiency increases because people are enabled to put more into their work. We shall also be rewarded by finding that the working lives of those for whom we are responsible have become rather more worthwhile.

APPENDICES

APPENDIX 1

COMMUNICATION COMPLICATIONS

Reporting negotiations

The rapid communication of results of negotiations between management and the trade unions on hours, pay and other conditions, presents real difficulties. At present, the usual method in industry, commerce, and the public services is for the trade unions' representatives to tell their members what has happened. At some later date, a notice giving the bare essentials may be put up by management. Such arrangements are not adequate. Inaccurate stories get through, wrong explanations are given, and supervisors and managers hear the result from shop stewards. This is unnecessary, as there are better ways of communicating negotiated matters.

Many managers and trade union officials accept the necessity for supervisors and shop stewards being given the facts about what has been settled and what led up to agreement.

Furthermore, the view has been taken that, as a negotiation ends finally in a joint management–trade union decision to accept a particular settlement, there is then a joint responsibility for seeing that the result is communicated to, and understood by, the employees affected. On the basis of these two principles, a drill for joint communication to employees should be aimed at and discussed with the unions involved.

At the end of each negotiating session – whether a decision is reached or not – a brief statement is agreed by the parties outlining what has taken place. If a decision has been reached, the main considerations advanced by both parties may be briefly added.

This joint statement is duplicated in sufficient quantities to ensure that every manager, supervisor, trade union official and shop steward concerned receives an individual copy within 24 hours of the settlement. In large organisations or industries with scattered units this may involve faxing, telexing, or telephoning the statement to large factories, offices or departments, in order to have it run off locally. In the case of smaller units, it may be possible to send the necessary number of copies by post.

In either of these cases, the managers, supervisors and shop stewards receive their own individual copies by hand delivery in the factory. Trade union officials receive their copies by post in pre-addressed envelopes direct from the centre where negotiations have taken place. *Notices are not placed on boards nor are announcements made to the press until 24 hours after the meeting.* By this time, managers, supervisors and trade union officials should all have received individual notification of what has taken place.

These arrangements will not prevent rumour, nor a possible leak to the press, but they do ensure that all those who are likely to influence opinion – both management and union – receive an identical, authoritative statement from their headquarters officials about what has taken place. Experience has shown that, once most people know that there is an official and reliable way of hearing the result of negotiations quickly, they do not base their judgements and actions on rumour alone.

Explaining management decisions where formal consultation has taken place

This problem arises where management has consulted the consultative committee before taking a decision (e.g. a change in meal times, a change in production planning). Management then takes a decision; in the majority of cases, the usual procedure is to inform the consultative committee, whose members are expected to explain that decision to those they represent. As pointed out on page 9 this method is inadequate, particularly if management has decided to take action *contrary* to that recommended by the committee.

What should the timing be, bearing in mind the need to inform management and respect the position of the work committee representatives?

The most effective order for informing people in such cases is:

1 top management explains the decision to management, including supervisors
2 management explains the decision to the consultative committee
3 managers and supervisors explain the decision directly to all employees affected

Example

A company has consulted its works committee on a matter affecting individual employees, and has taken a decision. The next meeting of the works committee is on a Thursday. Satisfactory communication timing is as follows.

- *Monday to Thursday a.m.* Top managers inform their managers and supervisors by systematic team briefing sessions, and if necessary arrange for the distribution of a manager's brief. Managers and supervisors are instructed not to pass information on to employees until Friday morning.

- *Thursday p.m.* The works committee is informed of management's decision and the reasons for it: if the decision does not agree with the previously expressed view of the works committee, some additional explanation will be needed. The committee is also told that managers and supervisors will explain the decision to all employees and the co-operation of the representatives is sought.

- *Friday a.m.* Junior managers and supervisors explain the decision to their working group in briefing sessions.

- *Friday p.m.* Notices posted and/or news-sheet made available.

Communication in a crisis

In a crisis, and particularly if there is a stoppage, it is very tempting to adopt some new method of communication. This can be dangerous, because if confidence has been lost, the introduction of any new procedure may only make matters worse. It is, however, at the very time of crisis that face-to-face communication through managers and supervisors becomes vitally important. This is a strong argument in favour of getting the system of face-to-face communication by managers accepted beforehand as a normal way of explaining things that matter.

Communication across an organisation

Problems of communicating between departments cause difficulty. Such difficulties become obvious more quickly than problems of upward and downward communication. Actions that can be taken to overcome sideways communication problems are:

- encouraging people to go and see their opposite number and not just to write or telephone
- setting up interdepartmental working parties for particular jobs
- moving staff so that, by the time an individual becomes a head of a department, they have spent some time in another part of the firm
- holding management discussion groups at intervals—management training seminars fill this need as a by-product.

APPENDIX 2

CHECKLISTS: ACTION BY MANAGERS

Action by all managers

Personal example

- Have I sorted out priorities for what must be communicated? Is the definition of the subjects involved acceptable? If not, what is a better one?
- Have I a systematic method for explaining face-to-face all such matters to the next two levels of management or supervision responsible to me?
- Do my supervisors, each month, talk to their working group about these matters?
- Is the noticeboard satisfactory? Is it up to date? Is someone responsible for it? Are immediate and permanent notices separated?
- Have I got a newsletter? Do I need one?

Instruction

- Have I told all managers and supervisors responsible to me what is wanted from them on communication? Is it in their job description? Do they know when they should hold a briefing session and what matters they should talk about?
- Do they require training in order to understand their responsibilities, or training in the practice of effective speaking and running a briefing group or a briefing session?

Check

- Do I periodically check that communication is getting through? Have I a reminder system?
- Do I walk the job to check that what I *think* is happening *is* happening?

Action by managing director or general manager

Check

- Am I satisfied that departmental heads have a drill for face-to-face communication on those matters which cause people to give of their best to their work? Would it help to ask each departmental head to write me a note outlining how they operate such a system and how frequently it is used?
- Do supervisors in the offices and on the shop floor get their people together each month for briefing sessions?
- Are supervisors (including those on shifts) brought together by managers in briefing teams? Are they at least as well informed as the shop stewards?
- Have we a system of representative consultative committees for upward communication covering works, technical and office employees?
- Is there a publication readily available for all to read, which carries essential information affecting employees? A news-letter? Or a newspaper?
- Is there an arrangement whereby a management bulletin can be circulated to managers and supervisors whenever they need to be informed of the background to a decision or a negotiation?
- Is there a brief, written annual report for all employees?
- Is there an annual meeting on each site which employees can attend and ask questions about points in the annual report, or anything else concerned with the progress of the company? Should we appoint, perhaps for a limited period only, a particular person to be responsible for seeing that communication is being carried out adequately in the organisation? Alternatively, would a senior person in the personnel department do it part-time?
- Are there accountability charts available for all in the organisation showing who is accountable for whose performance?

Action by personnel officer

- Am I keeping a check on where communication is failing? Am I watching for evidence of failures from committees, courses, individual discussions, surveys, investigations and walking the job?
- Is appropriate training available for managers and supervisors:

in their responsibilities for communication; in the techniques of effective explanation and conducting briefing sessions; in the purpose and practice of consultative committees?

- Should I introduce a system of management bulletins?
- Have I approached the trade unions on ways of rapidly reporting negotiated decisions?
- Is there a drill for communicating management decisions on matters discussed in consultative committees which ensures people are informed of them in the right way?
- Do I act as the board's conscience so that when decisions are taken at senior level the communication aspects of the decision are not overlooked?
- Is there a handbook on conditions of service for office and works? Is it adequate and is there a method for keeping it up-to-date?
- Are there accountability charts that make clear who is the immediate boss of each person?

APPENDIX 3

SUBJECTS COVERED IN TEAM BRIEFINGS

This is a list of subjects that have been briefed by many companies. It is by no means exhaustive but neither is it suggested that your company use all of them.

Progress

Product sales
Market share
Planning
Trading position
Development of subsidiaries
Financial results
Contracts gained/lost
Circulation figures
Cost comparisons
Export sales
Competitors' products
Quality index

Waste reduction
Safety comparisons
Productivity figures
Safe driving awards
Faults
Holes punched
Budgets
Sales targets
Accident record
Order position
Company achievement

People

Appointments
Resignations
Promotions
Internal vacancies
Selection procedure
Relocation of personnel
Overtime levels
Time-keeping
Company visits
Customer visits
Absenteeism
Long service awards

Labour turnover
Grievance/disciplinary
    procedures
Training courses attendance
Job security
Attendance at union branch
    meetings
Research into foreman
    selection
Management development
    programme
Conference plans

Policy

Legislation
Change in procedures
Supervisor development
    programme
Expansion plans
Capital investment
    programme
New committees formed
Advertising policy
Employee purchase plan
Setting up of new division
Industrial relations statement

Factory
    reorganisation/extension
    plans
Job evaluation exercise
Employee saving scheme
Drivers insurance
Suppliers hold-ups
Short-time working
New product information
Project reports
Long/short-term company
    objectives
Training courses

Points for action

Explanations of efficiency
    monitoring system
Fulfilling orders quickly
Sub-contractors on-site
Emergency procedure
Suggestion scheme
Heating, ventilation system
Accident reporting
Fire prevention
Start up after annual break
Stock shrinkage
Private phone calls

Car parking
Dealing with VAT
Maintenance priorities
Production of invoices
Increased costs
Stock discrepancies
Shortage of raw materials
Dealing with complaints
Non-decisions
Correcting of 'grapevine'
    rumours